FOR JC

C000139398

THE L.
TOP TEN

57 MILES ON AN ARDUOUS
BUT CHALLENGING WALK
OVER THE TEN HIGHEST
PEAKS IN THE LAKE DISTRICT
ON A CIRCULAR WALK
OR IN FOUR INDIVIDUAL SECTIONS

CAN YOU MEET THE CHALLENGE?

AN
ESSENTIAL GUIDE TO
HELP YOU COMPLETE
THE
LAKELAND TOP TEN

BY
BRIAN SMAILES

Other books by the Same Author :-

THE NATIONAL 3 PEAKS WALK
MARCH 1996
ISBN 0-9526900-2-0

THE NOVICES GUIDE TO THE
YORKSHIRE 3 PEAKS WALK
OCTOBER 1995
ISBN 0-9526900-0-4

THE NOVICES GUIDE TO THE LYKE WAKE WALK
DECEMBER 1994
ISBN 0-9526900-1-2

BRIAN SMAILES

A record was established by him in June 1995 when he completed 5 continuous crossings of the Lyke Wake Walk across the North York Moors in 85 hours, 50 minutes, a total of 210 miles over rough terrain.

ISBN 0 9526900-3-9

First Published October 1997
CHALLENGE PUBLICATIONS
P. O. Box No. 132 Barnsley. S71 5YX

CONTENTS

Front Cover: The Author at Scafell Pike Summit

PLATES

ACKNOWLEDGMENTS

It is with thanks to the following people that this book has been published:-

The expedition team consisting of Chris Barber, Graham Fish and Brian Smailes.

Geoff Whittaker for help in the research of information.

Graham Fish for his expertise in route planning, topographical recognition and in the checking of the technical details contained in the book.

The equipment suppliers for the expedition:-

    Buffalo U.K. Ltd., Sheffield - Sleeping Bag,

    Pulse 8 Fleece Clothing from B-Line Clothing, Wath-on-Dearne, Rotherham
    Fleece, Trousers, Gloves and Balaclava.

    Vango (Scotland) Ltd. - Vango Vega Tent.

INTRODUCTION

The Smailes' Lakeland Top Ten Challenge Walk is without a doubt hard but the goal is attainable.

The Walk consists of 57 miles of walking with over 30,100 feet of climbing. *(Plate 6).* The views are tremendous and the terrain in many parts inhospitable.

Once you attain the summit of each peak you achieve a sense of accomplishment as well as aching legs and limbs. Maximising as much natural daylight as possible it is best to ascend between Easter and October.

This guide is in two sections, the first details the walk split into four groups. Each group can be done in one day. The second is in one complete circular walk beginning at Bridge End Farm camp site and lasting approximately four to six days, camping on route and backpacking throughout. The book is laminated and compact enough to be carried on route along with the relevant maps recommended.

All compass bearings contained herein are given as magnetic and set in 1997. Magnetic north is estimated at 5° west of grid north in 1997 decreasing by about $1/_2$° in four years. Check new maps for future guidance.

Clothing and equipment for this walk should be adequate and of reasonable quality. It should be capable of protecting you, the walker from the elements and be robust enough to stand reasonable wear and tear. *(Plate 25).*

A good understanding of map and compass use is required as much of the route is remote and unpopulated. To get lost in these mountains is dangerous therefore respect for the outdoor environment must always be given and care taken.

The in depth planning required to complete the Lakeland Top Ten cannot be underestimated and the author cannot emphasise enough the effort required to complete the task by walkers of any age.

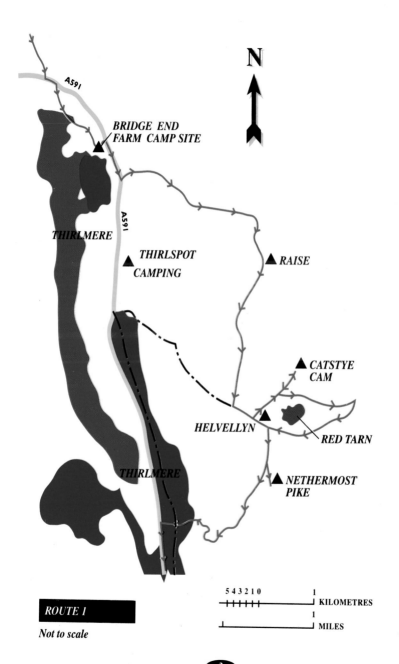

N

BRIDGE END
FARM CAMP SITE

A591

A591

THIRLMERE

THIRLSPOT
CAMPING

▲ RAISE

▲ CATSTYE
CAM

HELVELLYN

RED TARN

THIRLMERE

▲ NETHERMOST
PIKE

5 4 3 2 1 0   1
├┼┼┼┼┼┤   ┤ KILOMETRES

                 1
├───────────────┤ MILES

ROUTE 1

Not to scale

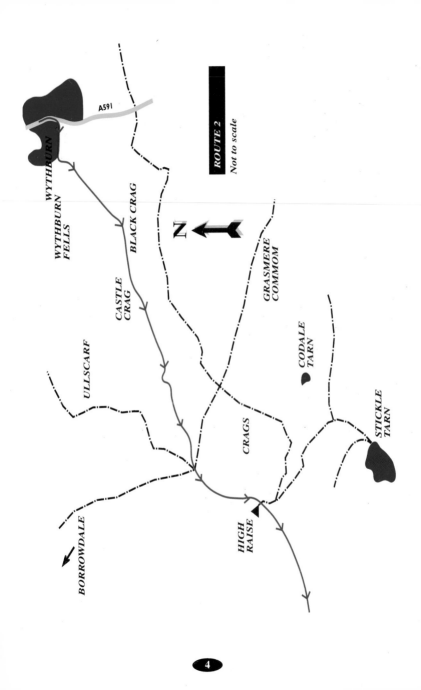

ROUTE 2
Not to scale

N

WYTHBURN
WYTHBURN
FELLS

A591

BLACK CRAG

CASTLE
CRAG

ULLSCARF

GRASMERE
COMMOM

CODALE
TARN

CRAGS

STICKLE
TARN

BORROWDALE

HIGH
RAISE

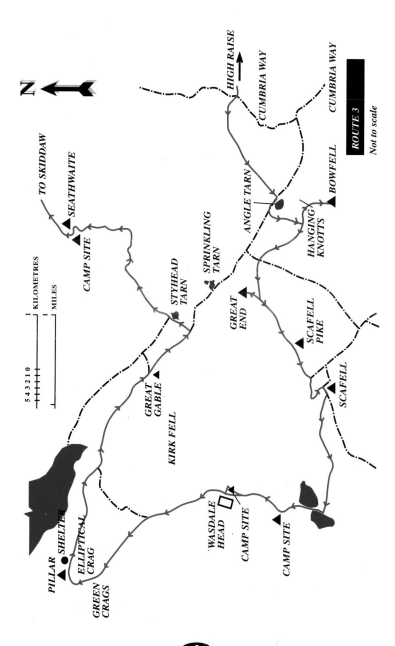

N

TO SKIDDAW

SEATHWAITE

CAMP SITE

KILOMETRES
1

MILES
1

5 4 3 2 1 0

STYHEAD
TARN

SPRINKLING
TARN

GREAT
GABLE

KIRK FELL

GREAT
END

HIGH RAISE

CUMBRIA WAY

CUMBRIA WAY

ANGLE TARN

BOWFELL

HANGING
KNOTTS

ROUTE 3
Not to scale

SCAFELL
PIKE

SCAFELL

PILLAR

SHELTER

ELLIPTICAL
CRAG

GREEN
CRAGS

WASDALE
HEAD

CAMP SITE

CAMP SITE

5

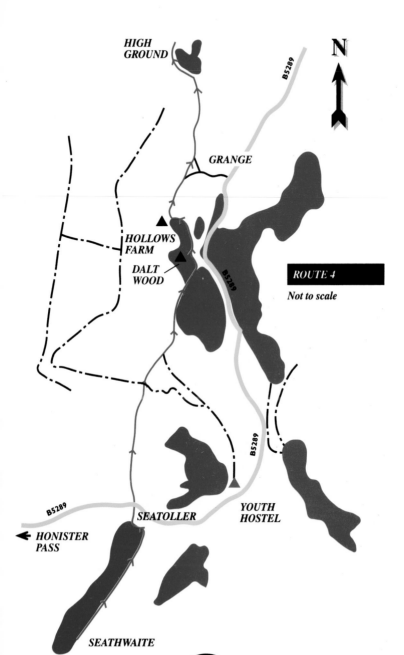

N

HIGH
GROUND

B5289

GRANGE

HOLLOWS
FARM

DALT
WOOD

B5289

ROUTE 4

Not to scale

B5289

B5289

SEATOLLER

YOUTH
HOSTEL

HONISTER
PASS

SEATHWAITE

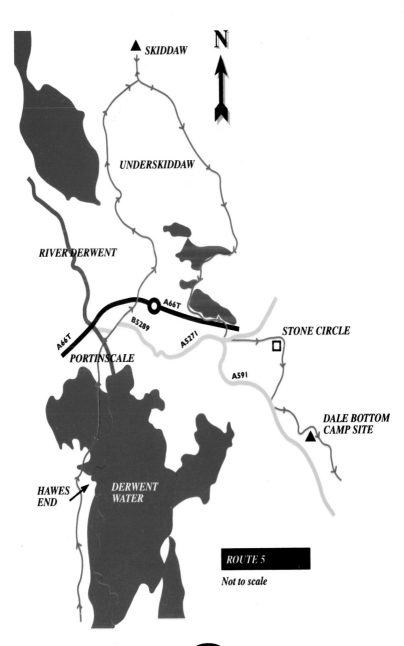

N

SKIDDAW

UNDERSKIDDAW

RIVER DERWENT

A66T

B5289

A66T

A5271

PORTINSCALE

STONE CIRCLE

A591

DALE BOTTOM
CAMP SITE

HAWES
END

DERWENT
WATER

ROUTE 5

Not to scale

THE CHALLENGE

This challenge incorporates a climb to the summit of each of the ten mountains. It can be started any time but it is advisable to start early to give you maximum walking hours in daylight.

Apart from the ten highest peaks there are two crags, Broad Crag and I'll Crag. Although these are not recognised as part of the Top Ten Challenge because they are both Crags and not mountains, the route still passes between them closely.

Because the crags are only 43 meters difference in height to Scafell Pike and within 700 meters from Scafell Pike summit the author has not deemed their inclusion necessary.

There are four natural sections to this walk, Skiddaw in the north west area, Helvellyn group in the north east area, Scafell group in the south west area and Pillar/Great Gable in the north west area. *(Plates 1 - 5)*.

When walking the full circular route, the walker should make use of recognised camp sites on route but depending on progress you may need to high level camp. In this situation be as unobtrusive as possible and ensure before you set off that you have enough supplies, water and the appropriate tent and clothing for the venture. Remember to leave your camp site as you found it.

Walkers may feel better able to complete this challenge one section at a time rather than the full 57 mile circular walk. Whichever way you choose you will find it exhilarating and worthwhile. Once all peaks have been completed, your official badge and certificate await you, details inside.

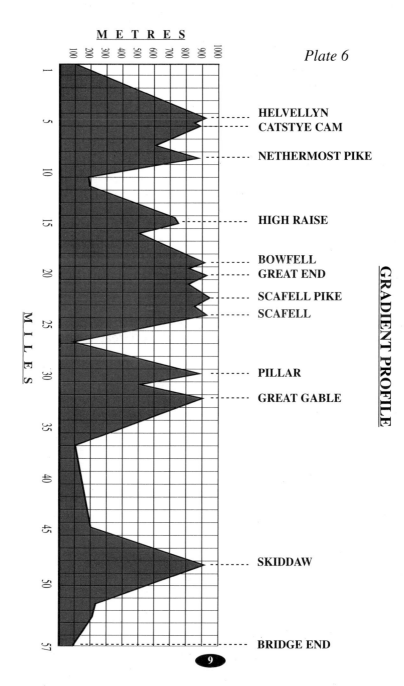

Plate 6

GRADIENT PROFILE

METRES

MILES

HELVELLYN
CATSTYE CAM
NETHERMOST PIKE
HIGH RAISE
BOWFELL
GREAT END
SCAFELL PIKE
SCAFELL
PILLAR
GREAT GABLE
SKIDDAW
BRIDGE END

9

WALK PREPARATION

It is essential that anyone undertaking this walk is prepared both in terms of physical bodily preparation and familiarisation.

BODILY PREPARATION

The route described consists of over 30,100 feet of climbing if you attempt the full challenge. To attempt this walk you should have a good degree of fitness. Even if you only intend to walk one group of mountains in one day, the fact that you are ascending some of the highest peaks makes it important to keep fit to enable you to complete the route safely.

Fitness training should incorporate leg muscle building and stamina training to help you in ascending mountains and maintaining a reasonable steady pace while walking .

Eating the right type of food both before you go and on your journey will help to give you energy. Items such as rice, pasta, potatoes, apples and bananas are all good sources of energy.

FAMILIARISATION

The route to be taken whether it be the full challenge or an individual grouping should be studied in detail. Walking times and distances should be looked at closely and a picture of the terrain to be encountered should be built up. This will prepare you better to complete your challenge.

A route card should be completed and a copy left with someone before you start walking. *(Plate 7).*

ROUTE CARD

FROM	TO	MAG/B	HEIGHT	DIST	TARGET	TIME

TOTAL TIME OUT = WALKING TIME + STOPPAGE TIME
ADD 30 MINS. FOR 300 MT. CLIMBED
WALKING SPEED 4KM/HR FOR MOUNTAINS

TIME OUT [   ]   TIME IN [   ]

LEADER ....

TEAM MEMBERS ....
....

Plate 7

11

EQUIPMENT

Walkers should already have a good knowledge of equipment needed for a walk like this and importantly how to use it, however, I feel it relevant to look at the technical merits and benefits of some of the clothing and equipment needed for this type of expedition. The following are items I used and the benefits derived from their use:-

Vango Vega Tent:-

This tent, although double the cost of similar size budget Vango tents is well worth the money paid for it. It is made from a thicker material than your average tent which is rip stop nylon. All seams are taped and the groundsheet is again made from thicker material than normal. It has a geodesic design and can stand up to very strong winds. The poles are aluminium as are the pegs and there are tension tabs at both porch entrances to keep the tent taut at all times in dry or wet weather. Either entrance can be used depending on wind direction. This tent served us well, is light enough to be carried and will sleep 3 people.

Buffalo 4 Season Sleeping Bag:-

This is one of the best sleeping bags on the market, it consists of 2 separate bags which can be fastened together inside to create a 4 season bag to keep you warm in the most severe winter conditions to -15°C The bag has a shaped body with a zip down the front. There is a hood with a zip on the outer bag so that all the body is enclosed and body heat retained. A comfortable warm soft bed is what you have when using this bag.

Maglite:-

A small sized torch but with a halogen bulb giving a bright light. The advantage is that it is light and compact, the disadvantage is that the batteries fade faster because of the halogen bulb burning brighter. Take spare batteries and bulb. The torch has a lifetime guarantee.

Trangia Stove:-

When walking the mountains described you may encounter gale force winds. This stove should enable you to cook in the worst of weathers and is light and compact to carry. Trangia stoves are fuelled by methylated spirits or by gas whichever you prefer. A minus point is the pan bases tend to get blackened.

Breathable Waterproof Fleece:-

This jacket from Pulse 8 consists of 2 layers of polyester fleece with a breathable waterproof lining. It is a new development in the Pulse 8 range of outdoor clothing and it is waterproof/windproof as well as being warm and light to wear. Deep pockets and a full length zip up front help give overall comfort. Prices for the complete Pulse 8 range of clothing are very reasonable and I can highly recommend them.

K2 Fleece Trousers:-

From the same manufacturer as the jacket, these trousers are made from very lightweight fleece, so much so you think you have none on! The material is polyester fleece which is water resistant and warm. They have pockets and a draw string at the front.

Fleece Mittens:-

Again Pulse 8 polyester made from the same fabric as the jacket. Very warm even in severe winter conditions. A must for those with cold hands.

Fleece 3 in 1 Balaclava:-

This is invaluable in snow, wind etc. Part of the Pulse 8 range of clothing from B-Line it has a draw cord in the top that can be slackened to allow the hood to double up as a neck warmer. When fastened it has a narrow opening for the eyes. This balaclava adequately covers the neck and keeps the head warm in the most severe conditions. I recommend it unreservedly.

Rucksack:-

This should be large enough to hold all your personal and safety equipment described. It should be robust enough to stand the test of putting on and removing in all weathers.

A rucksack should ideally have wide padded shoulder straps and a waist belt (on the larger ones) to stop it moving around. The material may be a type of polyurethane which has been proofed although it is advisable to put a liner inside to keep your clothes and other items dry in very wet conditions. Most rucksacks have a number of external zipped pockets in which to put small items and frequently needed ones eg. water bottles, maps, food etc.

The addition of draw strings to tighten and enclose the items in the main compartment securely from wind, rain and from dropping out is helpful and increases the versatility of the rucksack. Quick release plastic clip buckles to open or secure the top are also useful.

Survival Bag:-

It is usually made of heavy duty polythene and designed for a walker to get inside to help protect them from the harsh environment and to preserve their body heat.
It is a piece of safety equipment which may never be used but should be carried in your rucksack. *(Plate 9).*

Emergency Food:-

Chocolate, boiled sweets, fruit, nuts and mint cake can all help in providing energy and heat to the body when cold or in an emergency situation.

THE BODY

EYES
In winter snow goggles
are helpful.
Protect your eyes from
snow blindness and wind.

THE HEAD
Should be kept warm,
more heat is lost
from the head
than anywhere else.

THE BODY
Should be kept warm.
Build clothes up in layers
with wind/waterproofs
on top.

HANDS
Should be kept warm
with gloves.

MAIN BODY CORE
Temperature must
be maintained.

ANKLES
Should be protected by
wearing boots. These will
help stop you going
over on your ankle and
strengthen it.

FEET
Should be kept well
cushioned and dry if possible.
Good fitting boots will help
prevent blisters

Plate 8

SUGGESTED EQUIPMENT LIST

TENT / BIVI BAG
SLEEPING BAG
WATERPROOFS
RUCKSACK
WHISTLE
TORCH & SPARE BULB/BATTERIES
TIN OPENER
COMPASS
RELEVANT MAPS (LAM FOLD/WATERPROOF)
HOOD
GLOVES
BOOTS
EXTRA SWEATERS
PERSONAL CLOTHING
PENCIL/NOTEBOOK
ROUTE CARD
GAITERS
SPARE SOCKS
FIRST AID KIT
TOILETRIES
PLATE/CUP/CUTLERY
SLEEP MAT
WATER BOTTLE
SUNSCREEN
INSECT REPELLENT
FOOD
WATERPROOF MATCHES
STOVE/FUEL

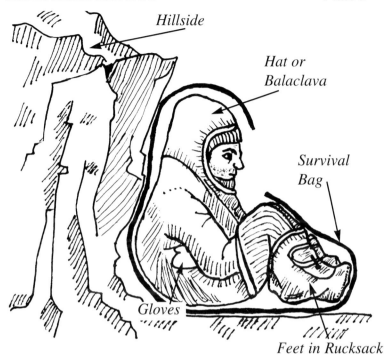

Hillside

Hat or
Balaclava

Survival
Bag

Gloves

Feet in Rucksack

To ensure the safety of you and the expedition team, you need to plan your route carefully, your equipment needs to be sufficient and able to stand up to the harsh conditions you could encounter on any of the peaks.

Details of your route *(Plate 7)* should be left with someone who can monitor your progress and more importantly alert the rescue services if you are overdue. Because you plan a route it does not mean you have to use it. Bad weather may cause a postponement or you may need to find an alternative route or walk. It is better to abandon if there is a problem than to risk lives ascending a mountain in atrocious conditions or badly prepared.

More accidents happen on the return journey than on ascents. This is due to a variety of reasons including complacency, exhaustion, lack of training, preparation and hypothermia. Many people do not realise that a calm sunny day in the valley can mean low cloud and gale force winds on the summit, add this to the wind chill factor and a walker badly prepared has got problems. Bad weather can sweep in quickly. This walk, particularly the full route over the 10 peaks is not for the inexperienced or the feint hearted.

Only walk routes which are within the capability of your party. One of the most common problems that lead to accidents is walkers getting separated from each other. There should be a party leader and that person should ensure the group walks at a sensible pace. Usually this is the speed of the slowest walker. Each person should carry a map and compass and know how to use them. A route card *(Plate 7)* should be carried by each person and they should all have been involved in drawing up the route beforehand.

Finally on mountain safety, be safe, stay together and be seen, take the right equipment for the task and walk carefully.

THE MOUNTAIN CODE
Initially:- Select equipment carefully.

Learn how to use it.

Be physically fit.

Know how to use a map and compass.

Where possible make an early start allowing time later in the day for bad weather.

Plan an alternative route for bad weather if possible.

Keep together.

Fill in route card and give a copy to a responsible person before you leave.

Check weather forecast.

WEATHER FORECASTS

The importance of predicting the weather pattern before you ascend each peak can be vital to the success or failure of you and your team.

It is advisable to listen to the forecast on local radio if possible for the area you are in.

Calm still weather in the valley can be gale force winds on the peaks, check your forecast before you ascend, are you liable to encounter low cloud, heavy rain, snow or scorching sun on your journey? Usually the forecast will help in deciding what and how much extra clothing you need to take with you and equally whether you need suntan cream and extra fluid.

It is essential not only to listen to the forecast but to write down and remember it. You can then plan your day to make the best use of the winds and your walking time, e.g. a circular walk or walking with the wind behind you.

When walking in mountainous country you can often tell if there is or will be a deterioration in the weather by the onset of low cloud around the peaks. Before this happens check your present position and look in the direction you are intending to go as far as you can see. Take a bearing with your compass then follow that bearing through the cloud to your intended destination using both map and compass where necessary. Never be caught unawares, when you reach that spot look again as far as you can see, take your bearing again then proceed as before.

Where conditions are very bad only those with a great amount of experience should be on the mountains. In virtually every type of situation like this it may be better to abandon the attempt than to risk lives on dangerous peaks. A careful look at the weather forecast could avoid disappointment due to bad weather.

The Lake District National Park operate a weather line on a 24 hour service. It is advisable to telephone before you set off to check on current conditions. **Tel: 017687 75757**

HYPOTHERMIA

Hypothermia is caused when the body core temperature falls below 35°C. If a walker is not properly prepared for the conditions or the equipment/clothing is not satisfactory then a combination of the cold, wet, exhaustion and the wind chill factor can give a walker hypothermia. *(Plate 9)*.

The signs and symptoms in descending order are:-
Shivering
Cold, pale and dry skin
Low body temperature
Irrational behaviour
A gradual slip into unconsciousness
Pulse and respiratory rate slow
Difficulty in detecting breathing and pulse when unconscious
Death

When on expedition there are ways of preventing hypothermia:-

1. Take extra sweaters to put on when cold.

2. Have suitable wind/waterproofs with you.

3. Build up body clothing in thin layers, adding on or taking off as necessary.

4. Take some food/hot drink or boiled sweets which produce energy and heat during digestion.

5. Wear balaclava/woolly hat to insulate the head, also gloves on hands. *(Plate 8 and Plate 25)*.

6. Shelter out of wind.

7. Take survival bag and if conditions dictate, use it. *(Plate 9)*.

In any type of emergency/accident situation it is always advisable to get off the mountain as soon as possible even in fog, snow or other bad conditions. The temperature difference between the valley and the summit can be several degrees. If the injured walker is able to move safely, going down the mountain is usually the best solution.

When conditions do not permit movement and if you are in a sheltered area, stay where you are until such time as conditions improve. It may be at this time that you put on extra clothing and use survival bags. *(Plate 8 - 9).*

Treatment for Hypothermia

1.   Provide extra clothing and shelter from the elements.

2.   Bodily warmth of others helps in a gradual warming.

3.   If well enough come down into warmer sheltered area.

4.   Give hot drinks if possible.

5.   Give chocolate or sweets if the patient can still take food.

6.   Do not rub the skin or use hot water bottle as this can cause a surge of blood from the central body core to the surface, this could prove fatal.

7.   The casualty should be placed so that the head is slightly lower than the body.

Alcohol should not be consumed on any walk and should not be given to anyone who has hypothermia. The body temperature will be lowered as well as giving a false sense of security.

GRID REFERENCES

As a walker you will find it necessary at some time to either find a place from a given grid reference or to make a grid reference from a place on a map.

All maps have grid lines running North/South and East/West. These are called "Eastings" and "Northings" and these lines have numbers on them. They can be further split into tenths, the numbers range from 00 to 99.

Grid references are normally given in six figures. The first three figures indicate how far to the East the place is. The second three figures indicate how far to the North the place is.

When making a grid reference look from left to right on a map and read the numbers going from left to right, write the numbers for the grid line to the left of your position, estimate the tenths to your position and write that number down to make 3 numbers.

Now look up your map and write the two numbers from the line just below your position. Repeat the second sequence as above. You should now have six numbers.

They are usually written as (example: G.R. 647556).

In using this method you should be able to pinpoint your target or position quite accurately on a 1:25000 scale map. Before you ascend the peaks you need to practice until you can both find grid reference points on a map and create a grid reference from a given position e.g. the grid reference for the car park near Wythburn on O.S. map 5 is G.R. 325136 check this then practice yourself.

GROUP 1
Helvellyn, Catstye Cam, Nethermost Pike Circular Walk
Time to allow 11 1/2 Hours
Total Distance 14.8 miles 23.8 Kilometres
Start G.R. 315192

Leave Bridge End farm camp site G.R. 315192, turn right to the main road *(Plate 10)* and right again on the A591 for just under 650 meters before turning left at the junction towards St. Johns In The Vale. The path you take is the narrow metalled road signposted Glenridding via Sticks Pass. The metalled road starts to ascend up past Stybeck caravan site with a farm building on your left. Ahead is a sign to Sticks Pass near some steps over a stone wall. Go up a steep grass path ascending to a farm gate with a large outcrop of rock behind it.

Go through the gate and over the stile following the path up and through another gate then over a small water channel. Ahead is another small gate, go through then cross the bridge over the stream following the path upwards. A sign points to public footpath & Swales car park but take the path on your left (which is almost due east) not the one to the car park.

You ascend steeply now up a loose stone and grass path. A waterfall runs down a ravine to your left as you ascend. Once up the steep section you come to a slightly inclined grass plateau and the walking becomes easier. In front of you there is another steep section on the way to the summit of Raise on part of the Sticks Pass route. The path ascends in a clockwise direction to Raise summit which has a small stone outcrop on top. To the left of the summit as you approach you may see a ski-tow. The path immediately before the summit is steep with large stones scattered on the path. In the distance behind you can see Bassenthwaite Lake and Skiddaw.

Once on the summit of Raise the path is clear ahead of you 221°M. *(Plate 11)*.

To the left of Helvellyn is Catstye Cam and beyond Helvellyn is Nethermost Pike. After descending from Raise you drop down to Whiteside Bank then up to Low Man which is the start of the ridge up to Helvellyn. The path is very stony but obvious. *(Plate 11)*.

At the 'trig' point of Helvellyn retrace your steps a short distance to the start of Swirral Edge which is marked by a pile of stones. Extreme care should be taken. Bearing is 57°M from the stones looking towards Catstye Cam. This route has a lot of loose stones and can be slippy in wet conditions.

In the valley is Red Tarn. *(Plate 13)*. When descending Swirral Edge it is slightly easier to go down the right path as the left is exposed and more difficult. Once down Swirral Edge the path initially has a scramble but becomes easier up to the summit of Catstye Cam. *(Plate 12)*.

There is a fork in the path. Take the left hand path to the summit of Catstye Cam then on the return take the left path descending towards Red Tarn. The stony path changes near the bottom to grass and peat. *(Plate 13)*. Go over the stream and the path is ahead bearing 112°M. At the stream you may see a stone wall ahead. The path meets the stone wall, at this point turn sharp right to go along Striding Edge. The path is very undulating and stony with a steep drop off at each side. Extreme care should be taken, particularly in the latter stages as you ascend back to Helvellyn summit.

Looking across to your right you have a good view of Swirral Edge and Catstye Cam. In front the sharp ascent to the summit from Striding Edge can be seen.

On the summit of Helvellyn after leaving Striding Edge there is a memorial from 1890 dedicated to a walker who died here.

At this point bear 195°M towards Nethermost Pike, *(Plate 14)*. looking across to your right bearing 230°M you may see a valley, this is the direction to proceed on the Lakeland Top Ten.

The path to Nethermost Pike is very stony. *(Plate 14)*. You arrive at a fork in the path, keep left up to the summit bearing 165°M at the fork in the path. Just before the summit there are a number of piles of stones to guide you. There are often strong cross winds here. You may see Ullswater in the distance to your left.

When leaving Nethermost Pike retrace your steps to the previous fork in the path then turn left at the fork to descend to the main road in the valley. Alternatively on a good day you can take a bearing of 266°M from the summit to go gently downhill to cut the corner off, rejoining the main path some way down. This should be done only in good weather when it is safe to do so. Thirlmere is on your right as you descend and go around a rocky outcrop before the path reaches the forest. Just past this rock outcrop keep on the main right hand path rather than the small path to your left.

The path here is uneven to walk on with a lot of loose stone making awkward steps. As the path descends to the forest you come to a gate. A sign points to Thirlmere Swirls on the right, Wythburn straight ahead and Grasmere to the left. When you walk through the forest section proceed for 120 meters on the descending path then turn right towards Thirlmere Swirls. This undulating path is narrow in parts but provides an excellent forest walk where a variety of wildlife including rabbits and deer can be seen. Continue on this path through the forest for 4 kilometres to Highpark Wood car park at the end of the forest.

Walk to the road from the car park and then turn right towards Bridge End Farm camp site passing the Kings Head Hotel at Thirlspot and the campsite there. The distance walked from the car park to Bridge End camp site is 3 kilometres.

GROUP 2
Scafell, Scafell Pike, Bowfell, Great End Circular Walk
Time to allow 11 Hours
Total Distance 14.9 miles 24 Kilometres
Start G.R. 235122

Starting from Seathwaite there is parking available near the farm. Nearby is a small cafe and a trout farm. Your ascent via the Corridor route to Scafell Pike starts here.

As you start walking you go through a farm gate continue on the path. Follow the path to a stile and gate. Continue on the path into the distance going up the valley. Cross a small wooden bridge over the river. The path starts to ascend as you go up into the head of the valley. Following the course of the stream you come to a gate and stile. The path is undulating.

Cross the small but impressive stone packhorse bridge known as Stockley Bridge as you turn to the right. When you pass through the gate the path starts to ascend steeply. Go through a small gate between a stone wall, the obvious path bears off to the right.

Looking back at night towards Seathwaite you can often see a small light at the farm. This is a guide for any walkers returning at night by this route, especially in bad weather.

Approaching the head of the valley the path flattens a little. A waterfall runs on your right and the path becomes very uneven and turns slightly left between the head of the two hills. It is very important to keep the stream on your right because in extreme weather conditions there is a tendency to walk to the higher ground on the left then cross the stream onto the right side which is damp and boggy.

The path along by the stream is very uneven with large stones and is difficult to walk over. There is a cairn on the level area between the two hills. It may be surrounded by water in extreme conditions but it is a good route marker. The cairn is approximately 80 meters from the wooden bridge you see in front following the rough uneven path. Cross the bridge.

The path is now on the right side of the stream. In bad conditions it can be very wet. Walk up between the hills to another cairn on your left. Just past it cross the stream again still following the main path. There is a tarn on your left side called Sty Head Tarn, cross over another stream, the path is now better to walk on.

The path starts to divide nearing the head of the valley, it is important to head for the large rocks you see in front of you, the path in parts here is grass. You come to a Mountain Rescue first aid stretcher box.

Take a bearing of 108°M to pick up a path towards Sprinkling Tarn. Walk for 2200 meters past Sprinkling Tarn then just before Angle Tarn turn right up to Ore Gap. This is a short steep climb and can be wet in places. Once on the Col you meet the main path from Esk Pike to Bowfell. Turn left and follow the path and piles of stones to Bowfell Summit. It is very stony but straightforward.

Plate 10
View looking back to the start of the Lakeland Top Ten with Bridge End Camp Site hidden behind the trees.
Your path is in the foreground ascending to Raise. The A591 road is across the centre.

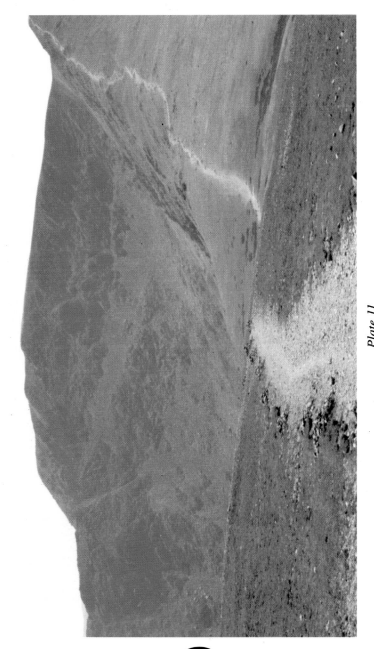

Plate 11
View of Helvellyn with Swirral Edge in front and the distinct path from Raise.

On descending Bowfell you may see Esk Pike ahead and Great End 3 kilometres behind it. The path is clearly visible. From Esk Pike summit bear 335°M and take the steep descent to the base of Great End. *(Plate 16)*. The path winds around the back of Esk Pike. When you ascend the path to Great End the path divides. Turn off right to the summit. The area is covered with small stones.

When leaving the summit retrace your steps and carry straight on now to Scafell Pike. You may see the round stone shelter on Scafell Pike. All the area is covered with large and small stones so extreme care should be taken. While ascending to Scafell Pike you pass between Broad Crag and I'll Crag. *(Plate 17)*. Immediately before the summit the path descends slightly before rising steeply up a shale path to the summit of Scafell Pike. The 'trig' point number is O.S. S1537.

Walking to Scafell the path is all stones as you proceed on a bearing of 247°M from the 'trig' point. The area immediately in front is called Mickledore then Broad Stand with a climb called Fat Man's agony. A stretcher box is situated here between Scafell Pike and Scafell at G.R. 210069. When at the stretcher box, Foxes Tarn descent is down to the left bearing 145°M. You can reach Scafell summit on this alternative path by descending to Foxes Tarn then ascending from the far side.

Your path to Scafell summit from the stretcher box takes you along the Lords Rake. *(Plate 18)*. This route is not suitable for anyone affected by heights. Extreme care is required as it is exposed in places and is a grade 1 scramble. Walk along the scree slope which is off to the right at the base of Scafell. Proceed along the Lords Rake $^3/_4$ of the way up the gully *(Plate 19)* on the first ascent.

Pass the large rock on the path then 2 meters further on turn left up the west wall traverse which is a grade 3 scramble with difficulty. *(Plate 19).*

On reaching the flat plateau bear right and Scafell summit is 100 meters ahead. Piles of stones mark the approach to the summit. Leaving Scafell summit walk on bearing 46°M around the cairn/shelter clockwise to Foxes Tarn. At Foxes Tarn follow a path around the crags to meet the path from Broad Stand descending towards Great Moss. Once on this main path descend to the southern foothills of Scafell Pike then turn left at the first intersection bearing 46°M for 1,100 meters on a path leading towards Sprinkling Tarn. You come to a stream on your left, bear 26°M and walk for 2 kilometres cutting across the main path between Esk Pike and Great End. Continue for 300 meters to your original path. At the junction bear left back to Sprinkling Tarn then Sty Head Tarn. Once at the stretcher box turn right descending on your original path to Seathwaite.

Plate 12
Looking down Swirral Edge from Helvellyn towards Catstye Cam.
The path descending to Red Tarn is off to the right.

Plate 13
Looking towards Red Tarn with Striding Edge running from the centre to the right.
The path from Catstye Cam is from the left just above Red Tarn.

GROUP 3
Pillar, Great Gable Circular Walk
Time to allow 7 1/2 Hours
Total Distance 8.72 miles 14.03 Kilometres
Start G.R. 187087

Leave Wasdale Head camp site and continue up the narrow road past the farm buildings in a northerly direction. At the last farm building turn left through a farm gate just before the house. A stone bridle path is in front. Follow the path and go through another farm gate. The stream is on your left. The path ascends initially steeply. Continue along the right side of a stone wall to a small gate with a stile at the side. Go over the stile and continue slightly downhill. The valley is in front with Pillar directly at the head of the valley.

You follow the general direction of the stream then turn up the left side of Pillar. Halfway up the valley the path divides and you take the left path bearing 324°M at the pile of stones which marks the fork.   Following this path you come to a small wooden fence with a stile which you go over and through a gate in a stone wall. Continue up to the head of the valley. The area is open grassland and undulating here. Bear left to start ascending Pillar. You will find no distinct path only grass then stone and scree further up. Work your way up to the top passing Green Crags on your left and Elliptical Crag on your right. It is a steep ascent in parts and can be difficult to ascend particularly in the latter stages. Eventually you reach the ridge then turn right on bearing 48°M to the 'trig' point which is 500 meters further on.

When you reach the ridge there are piles of stones and a windshelter near a cairn. The path to the 'trig' point is hard to define and there is a steep drop off to your left as well as to your right. Proceed down the rocks following a now more distinct shale path which initially descends then ascends up to the summit of Pillar and the 'trig' point. The area just before the 'trig' point is grass and stones with some cairns marking the path.

Follow the path towards Great Gable. In parts it is grass or stone and shale but well defined. Bear 125°M from the 'trig' point on pillar, walk along the ridge and descend the path before you start ascending to Great Gable. On your right is a tarn and a scree slope with a stream in the valley. At a gate on the path continue straight across on a direct route to Great Gable bearing 95°M. The path crosses a stream which runs down a ravine. Follow the narrow path around. Great Gable appears in front at 150°M. Continue along the side of the hill to a ridge leading up to Great Gable. When you come to the main path it is very rugged and winds through the rocks steeply to the summit of Great Gable. The final approach to the summit is covered in large stones. The path disappears and you have to climb up over the large stones to the summit. There is no 'trig' point on the summit.

Leave the summit of Great Gable on bearing 104°M at the cairn descending towards Sty Head Tarn. *(Plate 20)*. Walk for 200 meters then take bearing 143°M on a good man made stone path which descends to another main path just above Sty Head Tarn. When you hit the main path near the stretcher box take a general bearing of 209°M before turning right onto Toad How and passing Bursting Knott on a steep descent back to Wasdale Head camp site. As you walk down towards Wastwater, Great Gable is on your right. You may see Wastwater itself on your way down. Even at night the water reflects the moonlight giving you a guide back to the Wasdale camp sites.

On your descent back to Wasdale Head there are at least four other public footpaths which you will pass or cross on your way down.

Plate 14
View from Helvellyn to Nethermost Pike showing the distinct path up to the summit.
The path off to the right leads down to the A591 and Thirlmere.

Plate 15

Descending from High Raise towards Bowfell the path goes up the ridge in the centre then drops down to Angle Tarn before ascending to Bowfell then Great End.

GROUP 4
Skiddaw Circular Walk
Time to allow 7 Hours
Total Distance 8.45 miles 13.6 Kilometres
Start G.R. 262257

Leaving Applethwaite take the public footpath that runs from Applethwaite to Millbeck Farm in total about 1200 meters. Turn up through the farm buildings to Millbeck and Benny Crag and pick up the path that ascends steeply up to the summit of Skiddaw. You can follow the easy route from Millbeck all the way to Skiddaw on the Allerdale Ramble if you choose to. When you pass Carlside Tarn the final ascent to Skiddaw summit is very stony and steep. The presence of strong winds makes the ascent here more dangerous so care should be taken particularly from the tarn to the summit. The 'trig' point number is S1543. There is a wind shelter on the summit of Skiddaw.

Leaving the 'trig' point return on the same path for 650 meters then bear left at the fork in the path bearing 130°M at this point to leave Little Man to your right. The path here is stony. Further on you come to a stile, go over this then bear left descending to a car park near a forest. The path should be clearly visible in front as you descend. *(Plate 23).*

At the bottom of the hill bear right. Just before the car park a sign points to Skiddaw, Bassenthwaite and Mosedale. Go through a kissing gate and turn right to the car park. On reaching the car park turn right and walk for 2200 meters on the yellow 'B' road along the north side of the forest back to Applethwaite.

LAKELAND TOP TEN FULL CIRCULAR ROUTE

Leave Bridge End farm camp site G.R. 315192, turn right to the main road and right again on the A591 for just under 650 meters *(Plate 10)* before turning left at the junction towards St. Johns In The Vale. The path you take is the narrow metalled road signposted Glenridding via Sticks Pass. The metalled road starts to ascend up past Stybeck caravan site with a farm building on your left. Ahead is a sign to Sticks Pass near some steps over a stone wall. Go up a steep grass path ascending to a farm gate with a large outcrop of rock behind it.

Go through the gate and over the stile following the path up and through another gate then over a small water channel. Ahead is another small gate, go through then cross the bridge over the stream following the path upwards. A sign points to a public footpath and Swales car park but take the path on your left not the one to the car park.

You ascend steeply now up a loose stone and grass path. A natural waterfall runs down a ravine to your left as you ascend. Once up the steep section you come to a slightly inclined grass plateau and the walking becomes easier. In front of you there is another steep section on the way to the summit of Raise on part of the Sticks Pass route. The path ascends in a clockwise direction to Raise summit which has a small stone outcrop on top. To the left of the summit as you approach you may see a ski-tow. The path immediately before the summit is steep with large stones scattered on the path. In the distance behind you can see Bassenthwaite Lake and Skiddaw.

Once on the summit of Raise the path is clear ahead of you bearing 221°M.

Plate 16
View from the West side of Esk Pike looking towards Calf Cove and Great End.
Esk Hause is situated between Esk Pike and Great End in the mid right area.

Plate 17
Looking up to Scafell Pike between Broad Crag and I'll Crag.

To the left of Helvellyn is Catstye Cam and beyond Helvellyn is Nethermost Pike. After descending from Raise you drop down to Whiteside Bank then up to Low Man which is the start of the ridge up to Helvellyn. The path is very stony but obvious. *(Plate 11)*.

At the 'trig' point of Helvellyn retrace your steps a short distance to the start of Swirral Edge which is marked by a pile of stones. Extreme care should be taken. Bearing is 57°M from the stones looking towards Catstye Cam. *(Plate 12)*. This route has a lot of loose stones and can be slippy in wet conditions.

In the valley is Red Tarn. *(Plate 13)*. When descending Swirral Edge it is slightly easier to go down the right path as the left is exposed and more difficult. Once down Swirral Edge the path initially has a scramble but becomes easier up to the summit of Catstye Cam. *(Plate 12)*.

There is a fork in the path. Take the left hand path to the summit of Catstye Cam then on return take the left path descending towards Red Tarn. The stony path changes near the bottom to grass and peat. Go over the stream and the path is ahead bearing 112°M. From the stream you may see a stone wall ahead. The path meets the stone wall, at this point turn sharp right to go along Striding Edge. *(Plate 13)*. The path is very undulating and stony with steep drops off at each side. Extreme care should be taken, particularly in the latter stages as you ascend back to Helvellyn summit.

Looking across to your right you have a good view of Swirral Edge and Catstye Cam. In front the sharp ascent to the summit from Striding Edge can be seen.

On the summit of Helvellyn after leaving Striding Edge there is a memorial from 1890 dedicated to a walker who died here.

At this point bear 195°M towards Nethermost Pike. Looking across to your right bearing 230°M you may see a valley. This is the direction to proceed on the Lakeland Top Ten.

The path to Nethermost Pike is very stony. You arrive at a fork in the path, *(Plate 14)* keep left up to the summit bearing 165°M at the fork in the path. Just before the summit there are a number of piles of stones to guide you. There are often strong cross winds here. You may see Ullswater in the distance to your left.

When leaving Nethermost Pike retrace your steps to the previous fork in the path then turn left at the fork to descend to the main road in the valley. Alternatively on a good day you can take a bearing of 266°M from the summit to go gently downhill to cut the corner off, rejoining the main path some way down. This should be done only in good weather when it is safe to do so. Thirlmere is on your right as you descend. Go around a rocky outcrop before the path reaches the forest. Just past this rock outcrop keep on the main right hand path rather than the small path to your left.

The path here is uneven to walk on with a lot of loose stone making awkward steps. As the path descends to the forest you come to a gate. A sign post points to Thirlmere Swirls on the right, Wythburn straight ahead and Grasmere to the left. The path to Wythburn is the one which takes you down to the A591 road.

Once you meet the main road after descending through the forest, turn left walking for 700 meters then join the minor road on your right, a sign points to Armboth. Walk for 500 meters past a farm on your left to a stile on the left side of the road just before the bridge. There is a public car park on the right just past here called Steelend car park owned by North West Water. The path over this stile takes you on to your next journey up to Black Crag. There is a path on both sides of the stream. Take the first path not the second. The general bearing following the stream up the valley from the stile is 218°M.

Plate 18

The Lords Rake looking back and showing the path upper centre leading back to the stretcher box near Mickledore and Broad Stand. Care should be taken on this Grade 1 Scramble.

Plate 19
The path in the foreground leading to the Lords Rake. The left hand path along the West Wall Traverse is taken just above the large rock 3/4 of the way up.

Walk on the left side of the stream along the edge of the field. Go through a gate then the path in parts is stony and can be very wet depending on the time of year. Proceed up the side of the stream crossing a brook that comes in from your left. A narrow footbridge is in front, cross it then continue up the valley with the stream on your left side now. At the head of the valley you can see a picturesque waterfall appearing over the col.

The path ascends between Rake Crags and Castle Crag. Gradually the path begins to disappear as it gets lost in bracken in the final approach to the col, keep the stream on your left. On arrival at the top of the col you see a hanging valley with hills surrounding it. The area has numerous smaller hills and will probably be very wet. You will find it better to walk around the right side of the valley to the far end. This is because there are numerous small streams and wet areas.

In the distance ahead of you there is a peak called High Raise and the path to take you there is between the two hills in front of you as you approach the far end of the valley. The path becomes more evident as you ascend. At the top you meet another path crossing right to your left. Turn left here bearing 217°M to Low White Stones then on to the summit of High Raise. The triangulation pillar number is O.S. S5989.

Leaving the 'trig' point on High Raise take a bearing 223°M to bring you onto the path descending into the valley. You may see Angle Tarn 4 kilometres in front of you and the path leading to it is quite evident. *(Plate 15)*. On your journey you cross the Cumbria Way 2500 meters before you reach Angle Tarn. Pick up a distinct path to Angle Tarn then Bowfell.*(Plate 15)*.

When walking you may see Great End off to your right and Bowfell in front. Angle Tarn is situated just in front of the crags known as Hanging Knotts.

When approaching Angle Tarn you will not see it until you are close as it is hidden from view with the lie of the land although the path to it is quite evident.

A distinct path takes you around the side of Angle Tarn up to Bowfell. Follow this path then turn off left to ascend to Bowfell summit. This is a steep climb that can be wet in places. Once you reach the col called Ore Gap above Hanging Knotts that leads from Esk Pike to Bowfell turn left here and follow the path and piles of stones to Bowfell summit. It is very stony but straightforward.

On descending Bowfell you may see Esk Pike ahead and Great End 3 kilometres behind it. The path is clearly visible. From Esk Pike summit bear 335°M and take the steep descent to the base of Great End. *(Plate 16)*. The path winds around the back of Esk Pike. When you ascend the path to Great End the path divides. Turn off right to the summit. The area is covered with small stones.

When leaving the summit retrace your steps and carry straight on now to Scafell Pike. You may see the round stone shelter on Scafell Pike. All the area is covered with large and small stones so extreme care should be taken. While ascending to Scafell Pike you pass between Broad Crag and I'll Crag. *(Plate 17)*. Immediately before the summit the path descends slightly before rising steeply up a shale path to the summit of Scafell Pike. The 'trig' point number is O.S. S1537.

Walking to Scafell the path is all stones as you proceed on a bearing of 247°M from the 'trig' point. The area immediately in front is called Broad Stand with a climb called Fat Man's Agony. A stretcher box is situated here between Scafell Pike and Scafell at G.R. 210069. When at the stretcher box Foxes Tarn descent is down to the left bearing 145°M. You can reach Scafell summit on this alternative path by descending to Foxes Tarn then ascending from the far side.

Plate 20
Looking down to Sty Head Tarn from Great Gable with low cloud in the distance.

Plate 21
View showing the distinct path from Sty Head Tarn descending to Seathwaite. To the right is Stockley Bridge.

Your path to Scafell summit from the stretcher box takes you along the Lords Rake. *(Plate 18)*. This route is not suitable for anyone affected by heights. Extreme care is required as it is exposed in places and is a grade 1 scramble.

Go along the scree slope which is off to the right at the base of Scafell. Proceed along the Lords Rake $^3/_4$ of the way up the gulley on the first ascent. *(Plate 19)*. Pass the large rock on the path then 2 metres further on turn left up the west wall traverse. This is a grade 3 scramble with difficulty.

On reaching the flat plateau bear right and Scafell summit is 100 metres ahead. Piles of stones mark the approach to the summit. Leaving Scafell summit walk on bearing 291°M towards Green How and Wastwater. A path of scree which is steep in places will take you down with care to Wasdale Head.

Continue on the path along the ridge until you get to the forest known as Fence Wood. Join the path leading to Wasdale Head. This path will bring you to the main road and the lower camp site at Brackenclose near Wastwater. Here you can camp or go up the road for 1500 metres to Wasdale Head camp site. This is a convenient refreshment stop near the inn which provides both food and drink.

Leave Wasdale Head camp site and continue up the narrow road past the farm buildings in a northerly direction. At the last farm building turn left through a farm gate just before the house. A stone bridle path is in front. Follow the path and go through another farm gate. The stream is on your left and the path ascends initially steeply. Continue along the right side of a stone wall to a small gate with a stile at the side. Go over the stile and continue slightly downhill. The valley is in front with Pillar directly at the head of the valley.

You follow the general direction of the stream then turn up the left side of Pillar. Halfway up the valley the path divides and you take the left path bearing 324°M at the pile of stones which marks the fork. Following this path you come to a small wooden fence with a stile which you go over and through a gate in a stone wall. Continue up to the head of the valley. The area is open grassland and undulating here. Bear left to start ascending Pillar. You will find no distinct path only grass then stone and scree further up. Work your way up to the top passing Green Crags on your left and Elliptical Crag on your right. It is a steep ascent in parts and can be difficult to ascend particularly in the latter stages. Eventually you reach the top then turn right on bearing 48°M to the 'trig' point 500 metres further on.

When you reach the ridge on the top there are piles of stones and a windshelter near a cairn. The path to the 'trig' point is hard to define and there is a sheer drop off to your left as well as to your right. Proceed down the rocks following a now more distinct shale path which initially descends then ascends up to the summit of Pillar and the 'trig' point. The area just before the 'trig' point is grass and stones with some cairns marking the path.

Follow the path towards Great Gable. In parts it is grass or stone and shale but well defined. Walk along the ridge and descend the path before you start ascending to Great Gable. On your right is a tarn and a scree slope, with a stream in the valley. At a gate on the path continue straight across on a direct route to Great Gable bearing 95°M. The path crosses a stream which runs down a ravine. Follow the narrow path around and Great Gable appears in front at 150°M. Continue along the side of the hill to a ridge leading up to Great Gable. When you come to the main path it is very rugged and winds through the rocks steeply to the summit of Great Gable. The final approach to the summit is covered in large stones. The path disappears and you have to climb up over the large stones to the summit. There is no 'trig' point on the summit.

Plate 22
Looking across Derwent Water with Keswick in the foreground and the Allerdale ramble on the far side of the lake.

Plate 23
Looking back to Skiddaw showing the distinct path descending to near 'Whit Beck'.

Leave the summit of Great Gable on bearing 104°M descending to Sty Head Tarn. *(Plate 20)*. Walk for 200 metres then take bearing 143°M on a good man made stone path which descends to another main path just above Sty Head Tarn. When you hit the main path near the stretcher box take a bearing of 39°M and follow this main path right down the valley to the pack horse bridge known as Stockley Bridge then on to Seathwaite. *(Plate 21)*. Much of the path is man made and is prominent right to Seathwaite apart from one short section just as you cross the stream halfway down the valley.

Camping is available at Seathwaite where there is a cafe and refreshments available to walkers. Follow the path adjacent to the road from Seathwaite to Seatoller Bridge. It is mainly a flat grass and gravel path. At Seatoller Bridge follow the route of the Allerdale Ramble towards Borrowdale in a general direction of 5°M. There is camping available at both Seatoller Bridge, Dalt Wood and Hollows Farm 2 kilometres further on. *(Plate 4)*.

After passing Grange in Borrowdale you walk on a minor road for 950 metres until you approach Manesty Park Forest. Turn left off the road towards High Ground skirting the forest then walk parallel with the road to Hawes End along the base of Cat Bells. *(Plate 22)*. At the cattle grid near Hawes End bear 26°M through the forest to Silver Hill and Portinscale. Rejoin the minor road then bear right at the junction to Crossings Bridge then Thrushwood crossing the B5289 and A66T. The route generally from Hawes End to Millbeck is quite flat.

When you approach Applethwaite take the public footpath that runs from Applethwaite to Millbeck Farm in total about 1,200 metres. Turn up through the farm buildings to Millbeck and Benny Crag and pick up the path that ascends steeply up to White Stones. Just past White Stones rejoin the Allerdale Ramble to the summit of Skiddaw. When you pass Carlside Tarn the final ascent to Skiddaw summit is very stony and steep.

The presence of strong winds makes the ascent here more dangerous so care should be taken particularly from the tarn to the summit. The 'trig' point number is S1543. There is a wind shelter on the summit of Skiddaw.

Leaving the 'trig' point return on the same path for 650 metres then bear left at the fork in the path bearing 130°M to leave Little Man to your right. The path here is stony, further on you come to a stile go over this then bear left descending to a car park near a forest. *(Plate 23)*. The path should be clearly visible in front as you descend.

At the bottom of the hill bear right. Just before the car park a sign points to Skiddaw, Bassenthwaite and Mosedale. Go through a kissing gate and turn right to the car park. Bear left at the corner of the forest and descend skirting the forest on the path known as the Cumbrian Way. Eventually you reach the end of the forest on your right.

Soon after a forest appears on your left known as Whinney Brow. Follow the main path descending for 400 metres. Before the main road turn left towards Forge Brow keeping to the lower path just above the by-pass. A sign states National Trust Land. You reach a gate and stile. On reaching another gate and stile the path is gravel and stones here.

Turn right where the sign points to Brundholme Woods circular walk. Go over the by-pass on the metalled road then turn left on a path descending through the trees.

When you reach a fork in the path turn left and go down to a kissing gate then over the bridge crossing the river. Turn right walking along Forge Lane past Forge Mill. On reaching the main road turn left on the A5271 then A591 east. Just past the sharp bend take the yellow minor road up the hill to the stone circle which is on your right at the top.

Plate 24
Skiddaw in the background with the distinct path referred to in plate 23.
Your route in the foreground takes you near Dale Bottom Camp Site.

Plate 25

Looking from Great Gable to Derwent Water. Be prepared for wind, rain and general extreme conditions. Hood, Gloves and Wind/Waterproofs are necessary at times. A map case is also extremely useful in bad weather. Clothing provided by Pulse 8 Clothing.

Continue past the ancient stone circle a short distance to a wooded area on your right. Turn right on a path bearing 196°M keeping the trees on your left.

Climb over three sets of wooden steps taking you over stone walls. A stone wall will be on your left as you walk. Go through a gate and pass High Nest farm on your left.

Continue over a metalled road and a cattle grid then through a farm gate with a tree on your right side. Go over a small stile and immediately right over a cattle grid to the main road.

Walk 50 metres on the main road downhill. There is a gap in the stone wall on your left. Cross this field diagonally to another gap in the stone wall. Continue on this path towards Dale Bottom camp site. *(Plate 24)*. When you reach the camp site farm building turn left and you come to a ford and a small footbridge over a stream. Cross the stream turn right and then cross the field. There are small yellow arrows denoting the path. You arrive at a stile then a narrow metalled road.

Turn left on the road and go up to meet another metalled road 200 metres further up. Turn right then you pass two houses then a row of houses on your right. The path now is grass and gravel but quite distinct. A path ascending off to your left appears. Go up and over a stile here. The mountain on your left is High Rigg. Continue to ascend and then go over another stile with wooden supports on each side. Go over the brow of the hill then the path all but disappears and you go through a wet area and then over undulating ground and through bracken to arrive at the road. You should emerge at the road at G.R.306204. An old rusty post marks the opening.

Turn left on the A591 and walk for 200 metres then cross the road. Walk diagonally across the field in front bearing 175°M to pick up a public footpath to Bridge End camp site. The field you cross can be quite wet at certain times of the year. You come to a metalled road which you cross then through the kissing gate.

Follow a path through a gate next to a stone wall and cross a side road. Keep near the stone wall on a flat path. Now walk between two stone walls to a stone building and then through a farmers gate. Go down a slight incline along the side of a field to a sign marked 'footpath'. A packhorse bridge is nearby. Cross it and then ascend to a stile. Follow the path up to Bridge End camp site. You have now completed the Lakeland Top Ten.

CONGRATULATIONS! YOU ARE NOW A MEMBER OF THE LAKELAND TOP TEN CLUB.

BAD VISIBILITY DESCENTS

During the ascent of any mountain care should be taken especially in bad visibility.

More accidents happen on the return journey than the ascent. It may be difficult to pick out the path of descent in low cloud or in darkness. In situations like this follow the bearings and detail below to ensure a safe descent from the summit.

Taking these bad visibility descents may not bring you to your desired destination but will ensure you get down from high ground in bad weather or other emergency to a place of shelter.

HELVELLYN

Walk from the triangulation pillar on bearing 304°M for 1750 metres, then on bearing 340°M for 700 metres. These bearings will bring you back on a public footpath to the corner of Highpark Wood G.R. 320167 then following the path downhill to the A591 road.

CATSTYE CAM

Walk from the summit on bearing 226°M for 500 metres then pick up the path on your left on bearing 87°M to take you downhill to Red Tarn. When on the path at the tarn take bearing 57°M on the path back to Glenridding.

NETHERMOST PIKE

Walk from the summit on a bearing 352°M for 250 metres then turn left bearing 209°M following the distinct path which zig-zags a number of times on the way downhill. The path skirts then passes through a forest before meeting the A591 road.

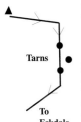

Tarns

To
Eskdale

BOWFELL

Walk from the summit on bearing 98°M for 300 metres then bear right on 180°M for 500 metres following a path downhill. At this point bear right on 235°M for 2700 metres descending to Hardknott and Eskdale.

GREAT END

Walk from the summit on bearing 220°M for 550 metres. Turn left on a distinct path bearing 84°M for 800 metres. Turn right on bearing 199°M for 2200 metres down hill towards Great Moss and Eskdale.

SCAFELL PIKE

Walk from the triangulation pillar on a bearing of 290°M for 200 metres. Look carefully for the path and cairns.

Walk for 300 metres on bearing 350°M
Walk for 250 metres on bearing 323°M
Walk for 300 metres on bearing 257°M

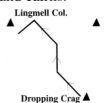

Lingmell Col.

Dropping Crag

This route takes you to the left of Dropping Crag and down to Lingmell Col and around to Hollow Stones.

Following this course from the summit should bring you off the peak and below the rocks in front of the Pike itself. From this point you can follow the path downhill to Wastwater looking for the cairns on route.

SCAFELL

Walk from the summit on bearing 269°M on a path descending to Burnmoor Tarn. From the tarn a gentle path can be taken to Wasdale Head if so desired.

PILLAR

Walk from the triangulation pillar on a bearing of 322°M on a distinct path leading to Ennerdale Forest. On arriving at the forest shelter can be afforded and a new route set.

GREAT GABLE

Walk from the summit on a bearing of 235°M descending on a winding path for 1600 metres before turning onto bearing 258°M then following this path for 2000 metres back to Wasdale Head.

SKIDDAW

Walk from the triangulation pillar on a bearing of 185°M for 550 metres then bear left on a longer but definitely safer path downhill on bearing 130°M. Taking the alternative path known as the Allerdale Ramble takes you on a very stony windswept and dangerous path. In reasonable weather this alternative path can be used particularly on the ascent.

IT IS IMPORTANT TO STATE AGAIN AT THIS POINT THAT ALL BEARINGS GIVEN ON THE BAD VISIBILITY DESCENTS ARE MAGNETIC BEARINGS. MAGNETIC NORTH IS ESTIMATED AT 5° WEST OF GRID NORTH FOR <u>1997</u> DECREASING BY ABOUT 1/₂° IN FOUR YEARS.

POST WALK

After completing your challenge of walking the ten highest peaks either individually or on one complete circuit, a souvenir cloth badge is available.

This is a colourful woven badge and depicts the Lakeland Top Ten. Send a cheque for £3.50 payable to E. Smailes and a S.A.E. to:

CHALLENGE PUBLICATIONS
P.O. BOX 132
BARNSLEY
S71 5YX

This official badge is only obtainable through Challenge Publications. A certificate stating you walked the Lakeland Top Ten is also available price 50p from the above address. Send a cheque as described above and a S.A.E. minimum size 23 x 16cm for certificate. Any factual account of your walk or comments long or short will be welcome. A regular updated price list is available from the above address enclosing a s.a.e.

Prices quoted apply in 1997/98.

USEFUL INFORMATION

WALKING TIMES
BETWEEN PROMINENT LANDMARKS

Bridge End Camp Site to Helvellyn Summit	3 Hr 40 Min.
Helvellyn Summit to Nethermost Pike via Circle around Red Tarn	5 Hr 30 Min.
Wythburn Car Park G.R.321130 to High Raise Summit	2 Hr 35 Min.
High Raise Summit to Angle Tarn	1 Hr 40 Min.
Angle Tarn to Bowfell Summit	45 Min.
Bowfell Summit to Great End Summit	1 Hr 50 Min.
Great End Summit to Scafell Pike	45 Min.
Scafell Pike to Scafell Summit	1 Hr 50 Min.
Scafell Summit to Wasdale Head	2 Hr 30 Min.
Wasdale Head to Pillar Summit	2 Hr 50 Min.
Pillar Summit to Great Gable Summit	2 Hr 40 Min.
Great Gable Summit to Seathwaite	2 Hr
Seathwaite to Hawes End	2 Hr 10 Min.
Hawes End to Skiddaw Summit	3 Hr 40 Min.
Skiddaw Summit to Stone Circle	4 Hr
Stone Circle to Bridge End Camp Site	2 Hr 20 Min.

NOTE: Walking the complete route will take approximately 41 hours walking time. This will depend on fitness of the group and the conditions encountered. It is suggested that 4 - 6 days should be allowed to complete the full route. Walking the 10 highest peaks in succession is a stiff task for anyone while carrying full equipment.

DISTANCES BETWEEN PROMINENT LANDMARKS
CALCULATED TO INCLUDE
ASCENTS AND DESCENTS

	Miles	Km
Bridge End Camp Site to Helvellyn Summit	4.83	7.77
Helvellyn Summit to Nethermost Pike via Circle around Red Tarn	3.71	5.0
Nethermost Pike to Wythburn Car Park G.R.321130	2.93	4.71
Wythburn Car Park to High Raise Summit	3.62	5.83
High Raise Summit to Bowfell Summit	4.17	6.71
Bowfell Summit to Great End Summit	1.99	3.2
Great End Summit to Scafell Pike	1.06	1.7
Scafell Pike to Scafell Summit via Lords Rake	1.02	1.60
Scafell Summit to Wasdale Head via Green How	3.19	5.13
Wasdale Head to Pillar Summit	2.98	4.8
Pillar Summit to Great Gable Summit	3.01	4.85
Great Gable Summit to Seathwaite	2.97	4.77
Seathwaite to Hawes End	6.28	10.1
Hawes End to Skiddaw Summit	5.8	9.33
Skiddaw Summit to Stone Circle	6.21	10.0
Stone Circle to Bridge End Camp Site	2.89	4.65

Walking the Lakeland Top Ten involves climbing over 30,100 ft and a total of 91.1 Km or 56.66 miles. This is a tough challenge for anyone therefore a good degree of fitness and navigational skills are required along with general experience of the outdoor environment.

USEFUL INFORMATION

HEIGHTS OF PEAKS	FEET	METRES
HELVELLYN	3117	950
CATSTYE CAM	2920	890
NETHERMOST PIKE	2923	891
BOWFELL	2959	902
GREAT END	2985	910
SCAFELL PIKE	3208	978
SCAFELL	3163	964
PILLAR	2926	892
GREAT GABLE	2949	899
SKIDDAW	3054	931

GRID REFERENCES

BRIDGE END CAMP SITE	G.R.315192
HELVELLYN	G.R.342152
CATSTYE CAM	G.R.348159
NETHERMOST PIKE	G.R.344142
BOWFELL	G.R.244065
GREAT END	G.R.226084
SCAFELL PIKE	G.R.216072
SCAFELL	G.R.207066
PILLAR	G.R.171121
GREAT GABLE	G.R.211104
SKIDDAW	G.R.260291

LAKE DISTRICT NATIONAL PARK WEATHERLINE
TEL: 017687 75757

RECOMMENDED MAPS

O.S. OUTDOOR LEISURE No. 4
THE ENGLISH LAKES NORTH WESTERN AREA

O.S. OUTDOOR LEISURE No. 5
THE ENGLISH LAKES NORTH EASTERN AREA

O.S. OUTDOOR LEISURE No. 6
THE ENGLISH LAKES SOUTH WESTERN AREA

All maps 1:25,000 Scale.

NEAREST MAIN TOWNS/VILLAGES

HELVELLYN RANGE - GRASMERE or KESWICK.

SCAFELL/GREAT GABLE AREA - WASDALE HEAD or
GRANGE IN BORROWDALE.

SKIDDAW - MILLBECK or KESWICK.

MOUNTAIN RESCUE POSTS

GATESGARTH (BUTTERMERE).

WASDALE HEAD G.R. 187088.

STRETCHER BOX NEAR STY HEAD TARN G.R. 219095.

STRETCHER BOX SCAFELL G.R. 210069.

CAMP SITES ON ROUTE (in Walking Order)

BRIDGE END FARM	G.R.315192
THRILSPOT, KINGS HEAD HOTEL SITE	G.R.317177
WASDALE HEAD	G.R.187087
WASTWATER	G.R.183075
SEATHWAITE SLABS	G.R.233122
SEATOLLER BRIDGE	G.R.245135
BURTHWAITE BRIDGE	G.R.257140
DALT WOOD	G.R.249167
HOLLOWS FARM	G.R.247171
DERWENT HILL	G.R.257234
CASTLERIGG SITES (2)	G.R.282225
DALE BOTTOM	G.R.296218

NEAREST TELEPHONE

BRIDGE END	G.R.318190
WYTHBURN	G.R.324136
WASDALE HEAD	G.R.187087
SEATHWAITE	G.R.235122
SEATOLLER	G.R.246138
GRANGE IN BORROWDALE	G.R.252175
PORTINSCALE	G.R.251236
APPLETHWAITE	G.R.264256
CAUSEWAY FOOT	G.R.293218

PUBLIC HOUSES ON ROUTE

1. KINGS HEAD HOTEL - THIRLSPOT
    Tel: 017687 73324
2. WASDALE HEAD HOTEL - WASTWATER
    Tel: 019467 26229
3. SWINSIDE INN - NEWLANDS
    Tel: 017687 78253
4. LYZZICK HALL HOTEL - UNDERSKIDDAW
    Tel: 017687 72277
5. TWA DOGS INN - PENRITH ROAD - KESWICK
    Tel: 017687 72599

LONG DISTANCE WALKERS ASSOCIATION
BRIAN SMITH
10 TEMPLE PARK CLOSE, LEEDS. LS15 0JJ
Tel: 0113 264 2205
This association is set up to further the interests of those who enjoy long distance walking. Members receive a handbook which details many long distance walks. it will also offer advice and information on most aspects of walking.

RAMBLERS ASSOCIATION
1 - 5 WANDSWORTH ROAD, LONDON. SW8 2XX
Advice and information on all walking matters.
Local groups with regular meetings.

LAKE DISTRICT NATIONAL PARK
INFORMATION CENTRE
GRASMERE - RED BANK ROAD   Tel: 015394 35245
KESWICK - LAKE ROAD   Tel: 017687 72803
SEATOLLER BARN - BORROWDALE   Tel: 017687 77294
GLENRIDDING - CAR PARK   Tel: 017864 82414

The above information centres can be contacted for advice. guide books and maps, accommodation and local weather forecasts.

GLOSSARY OF WORDS USED IN THIS BOOK

Alternative Route - *A planned route which can be used in difficult or emergency situations to bring you to your intended destination.*

Bearing - *A degree or number of degrees set on a compass then follow the direction of travel arrow to walk on that bearing to reach your intended destination.*

Cairn - *An ancient stone mound erected as a marker. Often modern day piles of stones are referred to as cairns. This is not the case but many people use this expression when referring to piles of stones that denote a path or route.*

Col - *A pass or Saddle between two hills. It provides access between one valley and another.*

Crag - *A steep rugged rock or peak.*

Escape Route - *Used for any emergency situation or in times of bad visibility. The main aim is to get you down to lower ground by the safest and quickest way.*

Grid Reference - *Derived from the national grid reference system. This is used to pinpoint a place on a map by the use of letters and numbers.*

Gulley - *A narrow channel or cleft in a rock face. Often has waterfalls and can be wet and slippy.*

Hanging Valley - *A valley which enters the main valley above the valley floor. Any river from the hanging valley may enter the main valley by waterfall or heavy torrents of water.*

Kissing Gate - *Swing Gate that usually lets one person through it at a time by moving the gate backwards and forwards.*

Magnetic Bearing - *This is a grid bearing taken from a map and the relevant magnetic variation added to it to obtain the magnetic bearing. See the relevant maps for details of current magnetic variation.*

Metalled Road - *Generally know as a stone chipping road. This term evolved and became regarded as the roads metal or the roads surface.*

Outcrop - *Part of a rock formation that sticks out from the main body of rock.*

Plateau - *A wide and mainly flat area of elevated land.*

Route Card - *A plan of action prepared before you leave. A copy to be left with someone so that if you fail to return by a planned time then help can be summoned.*

Scramble - *A climb or trek over difficult ground using hands if necessary to help movement.*

Scree - *A pile of rock fragments.*

Summit - *The highest point of a mountain or hill.*

Tarn - *A small mountain lake. Water from the mountains runs down and is caught in a land lock, so creating a tarn.*

Trig Point - *True name is Triangulation Pillar. These mark the summit of many mountains but not all the Top Ten have one. It is a small stone pillar with a number on it. The height of the mountain is taken from this point.*

NOTES

NOTES